In My Feelings Series

V O L U M E II

OTHER BOOKS BY ROBERT M. DRAKE

Spaceship (2012)
The Great Artist (2012)
Science (2013)
Beautiful Chaos (2014)
Beautiful Chaos 2 (2014)
Black Butterfly (2015)
A Brilliant Madness (2015)
Beautiful and Damned (2016)
Broken Flowers (2016)
Gravity: A Novel (2017)
Star Theory (2017)
Chaos Theory (2017)
Light Theory (2017)
Moon Theory (2017)
Dead Pop Art (2017)
Chasing The Gloom: A Novel (2017)
Moon Matrix (2018)
Seeds of Wrath (2018)
Dawn of Mayhem (2018)
The King is Dead (2018)
What I Feel When I Don't Want To Feel (2019)
What I Say To Myself When I Need To Calm The Fuck Down (2019)
What I Say When I'm Not Saying A Damn Thing (2019)
What I Mean When I Say Miss You, Love You & Fuck You (2019)
What I Say To Myself When I Need To Walk Away, Let Go And Fucking Move On (2019)
What I Really Mean When I Say Good-bye, Don't Go And Leave Me The Fuck Alone (2019)
The Advice I Give Others But Fail To Practice My Damn Self (2019)
The Things I Feel In My Fucking Soul And The Things That Took Years To Understand (2019)

For Excerpts and Updates please follow:

Instagram.com/rmdrk
Facebook.com/rmdrk
Twitter.com/rmdrk

ISBN: 978-1-7326901-2-7

Book Cover: Robert M. Drake

For The Ones Who Feel Like They've Lost Everything

CONTENTS

THE ADVICE I GIVE OTHERS BUT FAIL TO PRACTICE MY DAMN SELF

ROBERT M. DRAKE

EVERYWHERE YOU GO

All that you need
you carry

with you—you take
with you.

So if it is
a person

that you need.

Then let it be known
that when you

depart
you take

a piece of their heart
in your hands.

In your soul.

In your thoughts
and memories.

You take them with you
and have the gift

to love them...
everywhere you go.

Never take that
for granted.

A LITTLE HARDER

You just don't.

You fight for them
no matter how hard

it gets.

You fight with them
no matter what

ends up
happening.

No matter what
the outcome is.

You don't give up
on the people you love.

You just don't.

Doing so
will be something

that will eat you
alive

and you will never

forgive yourself
for not trying

a little harder.

You will always
wonder why

and what if.

And it will always
come back to haunt you

no matter who
you end up with.

No matter where you go.

No matter who you meet
and who you don't.

You don't give up
on the people

you love.

Period.

You just don't.

You give it your all

until there's nothing left
of you.

Until it kills you.

It is better to die

trying

than to live

knowing

you could have
loved

a little harder.

SAD PART

The sad part was,

I spent most of my life
looking for a love

I knew
never existed.

Chasing people
I knew

I didn't deserve.

And writing poetry
that didn't really matter

to anyone
but myself.

After all this time
the world is still

a very,
very

lonely place.

WISH IT

As long
as you wish it...

always know
that you can

start over.

That you can
pick yourself up

right where
you began

to fall apart.

That there's always
a new day tomorrow

and that you can
always choose

to love yourself
and chase

what you deserve
when you need it most.

As long as you

wish it.

As long as you know
what you deserve.

SOMEONE

Don't let them
turn you

into someone
you can't recognize.

Into someone
cold and cruel.

Into someone
who doesn't care

or love.

Don't let them
change you

or hurt you.

Don't let them
make you believe

that you are incapable
of love.

That you are
not worthy

or deserving of it.

You are so much more
and they are too.

It is just,
sometimes

we don't know
what we are capable of.

Sometimes
we don't know

who we are
or what we're supposed

to do.

Who
we're supposed

to love
and who

we're supposed
to let go.

But still,
don't let them change you.

Don't let them break you
or turn you

into someone else.

Believe
in what you have
within.

Hold it.

Harness it
for what it is—for

the light it radiates.

Your soul
is a star

and your heart
is a goddamn galaxy

waiting to be discovered.

And some people
are astronomers,

scientists of the heavens
and some are gazers

waiting to reach

the stars
but have no way
of going.

It is true.

Some chase the light
and some become it...

and then
there's you.

And you know
what exists

inside of you.

So keep shining.

Keep glowing
through the darkness.

It is
what it is

and you
just have to learn

not to change
for no one.

And if you do,
make sure

it's for the best.

That's all.

HUMAN

You have needs,
of course,

you're human!

Therefore,
you're allowed to break,

cry, and fall.

You're allowed
to go through

these things
because you know

what you deserve
and you understand

how these things
happen

in order
to be loved.

PROGRESS

You're a work
in progress

therefore,
it's okay

to cut any loose ends.

It only means
you're making space

for something new
to grow.

NEED TO BE LOVED

It's simple.

I need to be loved.
I need to be missed.

I need to know
that I'm thought of.

That someone
 is thinking of me

in the middle of the day,
even if it's

for a split second—wondering,
what it is

I'm doing
that very moment

and

if I'm thinking
about them

the same way.

NOT ONCE

I'm not
who I once was

when I was with you.

So how could you
return

thinking
I'd let you back in.

I'm different now.

I'm no longer
a flower—surviving

off the memories
of all the people

I've lost—feeding
off the things

that make it
easier to love

and get attached to.

I'm better now

and I know
it's hard to see past

what you remember
about me

but it doesn't matter.

I've spent
enough time

learning about myself
to realize…

how the people
who do you wrong

come back—
never really changing—staying

exactly the same.

And it's sad,
because you actually think

you belong here.

You actually think
you belong

beneath my skin.

Like I said,
I'm different now

and it's easier for me
to look you

in the eyes
and tell you,

no!

Rather than
to swallow my tongue

and watch you
step all over me again.

You are not
welcomed here.

I'm sorry
but I'm not sorry.

I've outgrown you

and I'm so much better
than that.

TO LOVE OR NOT

The truth is,
you've saved me
from myself

and in many ways,
you've made it

that easier
to love.

THE RIGHT WAY

Everything feels right
when I'm with you,

wrong when I'm not.

I don't know
what it is

but you fill me
in ways

I never thought
were possible.

In ways
I never imagined.

I love you...

a thousand times
all over again.

I love you...

with all that I am
and all that hurts.

I love you...

and I can't seem
to be myself

without you.

Nothing will ever
make any sense to me,

that is,
if it's *not*

including you.

FUNNY THING IS

You hate me
but the funny thing is,

I'm just like you.

I'm looking for hope
in a hopeless world.

For love
and peace.

For someone
who understands me,

someone
who makes me feel

a lot
less
alone.

BEAUTIFUL 2

You asked me
once

why does it hurt
so much?

And back then
I did not have an answer

but

I think,
now I do.

I think,
now I understand.

Because deep
within our souls

we have this
uncontrollable urge to love

and
to be loved.

It's in all of us.
It's simple.

The more you love,
the more you hurt

and the more you feel both...
the more you realize

how you can't

have one
without the other.

*To love
is to hurt.*

To love
is to be vulnerable

at all times—knowing

one day,
it can all fall apart

all over your hands.

And there's no way
around it.

This is what we live for...
for something special,

for that rare moment

that might
last long enough

to make us forget
how hard

it is
to live.

How hard
it is

to love…

but also
how blessed we are

to experience
the both of them.

The thing is,
we'll do it anyway,

even if we know
it might end

with a little pain.

We do it
regardless
and we'll keep doing it…

until our bones
are brittle

and our bodies
no longer have

the strength
to carry on.

We'll do it!

No matter how bad
it hurts.

No matter how tragic
our previous lovers

were to us.

We'll do it anyway.

We'll always
choose love

above everything else.

This is,
truly,

what makes
us beautiful.

NOTHING WRONG

There's nothing
wrong with you

or the people
you love.

You're not broken.

You're not empty
or crazy.

It's just
some relationships

aren't meant
to work out.

Some people
aren't meant

to be yours
and some

only come
into your life

to teach you
the importance

of self-love.

So take the lesson.

Live by it.

That's how
your healing will begin.

PUT YOUR TIME

Not everyone
will agree with you.

Not everyone
is going to see

eye to eye
with what you do

or what you feel.

But I will say this,
you're too damn young

to be heartbroken.

You should be chasing
your goals

instead
of chasing love.

You should be chasing
what you've always wanted

and following up
with what

you would have
told yourself

when you were much younger.

That is,
what your older self

would want
for your younger self

to do.

And I know
you love them.

I know
you've given up

on so many things
for them

but enough
is enough, right?

You tell yourself
tomorrow.

You keep thinking
everything will be okay,

that is,
if you give them time.

If you're patient
with them

but you're overlooking
the truth here.

You're overlooking

time
and how much of it

you have, here.

You're not meant
to live forever

but the least
you can do

is be happy.

The least
you can do

is chase your dreams
with or without

someone to hold.

You deserve to
and yes,

I'm not saying
to be alone

all your life.

No,
I'm not saying

you're not deserving
of love.

What I am saying is,
to work on yourself.

To love yourself.

To do
what you must

but only...
for yourself.

Then, God willingly,
you put your time,

effort, love,
dreams and hopes

into someone else.

To build with them.

To grow
and move forward

with them.

But only
if you're happy

with yourself.

If you've done all
that you can

for yourself.

You're the star
of your own story...

so keep your head up.

Stay strong
and remember,

you don't need
to fight

so hard for love…

unless

it's for something
or someone

you know
you deserve.

Stay beautiful.

TRY NOT TO

It's hard
not to get

attached
when you love them.

It's hard
to let go

when you feel
like you need to

especially,

for reasons
you can't change

at all.

You deserve more.

*Some people
just don't change*

*not unless
you do.*

DESERVE MORE

You know
you deserve more

but you never do
anything

about it.

The same way
you need to

move on
but you're too afraid

of what
might come

next.

THE PROBLEM

That's the problem.

Some people
don't own up

to what they do.

They blame others.

They hurt
and break other people

without understanding
what it is

they've done.

Without knowing
what it is

they're doing
to the people

they love
and themselves.

BENEATH WHAT HURTS

And I don't know
why it's so hard

for me
to talk to you.

Why it's so hard
for me

to open up
with you—to

tell you
what it is

that I am
really feeling.

I don't know why
the truth

gets so hard
sometimes.

Why the truth
hurts so much

and why the past

is something

so hard
to get away from.

I don't know why...
and it has nothing

to do
with the way

I feel about you.

It has nothing
to do

with what I want.

It's about me
and I don't want to lose

my soul
in the middle

of it all.

I don't want
to accept change

and move on...
but for you

I'm willing
to do

whatever it takes...

because

it's hard for me
to let go

of certain habits
and things

I've grown
accustomed to.

It's hard for me
to be

a certain way
with you.

Hard for me
to show you

how much I care
but I'm tired

of being cold.

I'm tired

of feeling empty
and numb.

I'm tired
of watching people

come and go.

Of drowning
within myself

and being afraid
of being alone.

I just don't
want to lose you

because of
the way I am.

I want to be different
with you.

I want to start over.

I want to let go
of my past

and begin
my future with you.

I'm looking forward to it.

I just want
to spend the rest

of my life with you
and show you

that beneath it all,
I still

have a good heart.

That beneath it all,
I still

have a chance—a shot...
just give it to me

and I will show you.

I will be
real with you

and hope
it's for the best.

THE YEARS

Throughout the years
I have learned

three major things.

I.

Sometimes bad things
happen to good people

and sometimes
you might think

you know someone.

You might think
they're on your side

but deep down inside
they're not.

Pay attention.

Actions speak louder
than words

and words

are just

another way
to cover up
the truth

with lies.

II.

Almost everything
we go through

we can't control.

That means,
if it's yours,

then somewhere
down the line

it'll return to you
and if it's not,

then you have to
make peace

with it
and move on.

It's as simple
as that.

And

III.

Letting go
is never an easy

thing to do.

No matter how many times
you've rehearsed it.

No matter how many times
you've played it

in your head.

It never goes
as planned

and almost always
does it sting

a little harder
than you thought.

THE SACRIFICE

Sometimes love
is sacrificing

a part of yourself...

letting go
of something

that just doesn't
fit with the relationship.

Sometimes love
is about that.

About adjusting
and reinventing

yourself

to make things work.
To make things

flow
a little easier.

And I'm not saying
to change

completely
but I'm saying

to let go
of bad habits.

To let go
of anything

that'll weigh
the relationship down.

It's not such
a bad thing to try.

It's not such
a bad thing

to accept.

Love is about sacrifice
and everyday

someone
is letting

a piece of themselves
go

for the people
they love.

I don't make the rules.

That's just
the way things are.

BAD TERMS

It's hard to trust
when you've been

lied to.

The same way
it's hard

to love someone
new

when everyone
you've ever cared

about

has left
on bad terms.

WHAT I DON'T KNOW

I know you've had
a hard

and troubled past.

I know you've been
through hell

and back.

And I know
you've experienced

some things
most won't

in their lifetime.

I know
it hurts

when you're alone.

I know it kills you,
burning at the back

of your throat—setting
your soul on fire.

I know
you have convictions.

Contradictions.

A handful
of questions

and not enough answers
to go by.

I know all these things.
I feel all these things.

But let me be
the first

to say that
I care.

Let me be the first
to say

that you're not
really alone.

That you're not
really empty

or broken
or weak

or numb
or lost
or confused.

Let me be
the first to say,

that you are *loved.*

That you are
thought of

when the days go by
when you've gone

missing.

That you're wanted
and needed.

That you are
so much more

than you think
you are.

Let me be
the first to show you

that you are
deserving of love.

Of gentleness
and softness.

Of being held
all night long.

Let me be
that person for you.

Let me be
that person

who stops everything
their doing

just to make

sure
you're okay.

Let me be
there for you.

Let me care
and protect your heart.

Protect your well-being
and energy.

Let me love you.
But let me

with all soul.

Let me
with all heart.

Let me
fall in love

with your laughter
and let me

silence what hurts.

I know
I'm someone

you deserve
and I know

I can
with honesty
and truth.

So let me
love you today

because tomorrow
is not promised.

Today
is already

a good day
because of you.

SPARE ME

I'm not asking
for you

to spare me.

For you
to save me

from myself.

For you
to help me

find
what it is

I've lost.

I'm not asking
for your attention.

For your time
or for your love.

I'm asking
for your friendship.

For your time

when I need it most.

I'm asking
for you

to be there
for me

when I feel
empty

and alone.

GROWING UP

Don't punish me
for caring

about you
and don't put me down

for being vulnerable
with you.

I'm not weak
for loving you.

I'm not stupid
for giving you

chances

and I'm not
naive for believing

in you, in us.

Yes,
I've got

a lot of
growing up to do

but that doesn't mean
I don't know

what I want.

That doesn't mean
I don't know

who I need.

I want you
and I'm willing to fight

for you.

Even if it kills me
or not.

Doing anything else
wouldn't make

much sense to me

at all.

SOULMATES

We might be
soulmates.

I think
I fell in love

with you

the moment
you said

hello.

HOW SAD

How sad.

To think
that you must

go through pain
in order to grow.

That you must

go through loss
in order to appreciate

what you have—who
you have.

That you must
get your heart broken

in order to recognize
love.

How sad.

To go through
all of these things

alone,

without anyone

preparing you
or giving you

the right amount
of advice

to carry on.

YOUR DREAMS

Don't believe
everything you think,

everything you feel.

Sometimes
the heart

is a liar.

Sometimes
the mind

plays tricks on you.

It makes you
believe

and confuses
your reality.

You're not
a loser.

You're not
behind your peers.

You're not delayed.

And you're definitely

not

what those
who are closest to you

are saying.

You're so much more.

Every atom
in your body…

is
so much more.

Every thought
and every feeling...

is
so much more—beyond

your doubts
and fears.

So enjoy your life
for what it is.

Take your time.
Make your own path.

Work on yourself
and don't be afraid

of what comes next.

Your life
is *your* life,

therefore,

you should never
lose sight

of your dreams.

SORROW

It's hard
to explain

and I don't
know why...

but almost
every day

I feel
as if I'm almost

in reach
of something I need.

In reach
of something

holy.

Something
out of this world...

and at the same time
it also feels

as if

I'm slowly watching
it slip away.

As if

I'm not
close enough

to catch it
and claim it

as my own.

That's love.

That's how it feels
when I am

with you.

As if

we were
almost there

but we arrived
too late

to comfort
each other's

sorrow.

What a terrible

way

to let
things be.

I HAVE GONE

Sometimes

I feel
like my brain

has a brain
of its own.

Like my heart
has a heart

of its own.

I think
and feel too much,

a thousand miles
an hour.

Always going,

always moving
and never stopping

to realize

how far
I've gone.

DAMN IT

And I'm sorry
for hurting you

while I was
hurting.

I just

didn't know
what I was doing.

I was selfish.

I was wrong
and I was thinking

only

about myself
and what

I was going through.

I should have
appreciated you

a little more
because now

you're gone
and all

I'm left with
is regret.

Damn.

LOSE YOURSELF

Yes.

It is true.

Pain really
does change people.

Pain really
does change

the human heart.

It can
make you

or break you.

There is no lie
in that

and I have felt
enough of it

to say,
that things

do get better.

That things
do sort themselves out

in the end.

Believe me,
you'll live through it.

You always have
and you always will.

Everything has
its reason

and sometimes

you lose people
while other times

you lose

yourself.

THINGS DWELL

And sometimes

you don't know
what to feel

anymore.

Sometimes
you don't know

where you stand.

Time goes
and so do

your feelings.

You watch them
float upwards

toward the moon
where all things

that are lost
go to dwell.

HURTS THE MOST

You were
the right one

for me
but you met me

at the wrong time.

You met me
while I was trying

to figure
myself out

and that's
what hurts

the most.

I carry this with me
deep within

my bones.

ORDER TO LOVE

It's hard
to not have both.

You can't have one
without the other.

You can't have

love
without some kind
of sadness.

You can't have

success

without some kind
of sacrifice.

And you can't

find yourself
without losing

a piece of yourself
in the end-something's

that meant

the world to you.

That's life.

It's a balance
between what you want

and what you need.

Between

what you're willing
to lose

in exchange
for what you're determined

to gain.

Between

who you're willing
to let go

in order
to love.

THAN MOST

You're going to
lose people

you thought
would always be there.

Some friends
you believed

would always
be around.

But I've learned,
in all my years,

people change.

No matter what kind
of history

you have together.

People change,
relationships change

and love changes.

That's life.

It happens to us all.

It is just
some of us

go through this later
while the rest of us

go through it
earlier than most.

REMEMBERED

Some people
will never understand

the chaos
in your heart.

The indecisiveness.
The conflict.

The unbalanced force
within you.

Because people
are not meant

to be understood.

They're meant
to be loved

and remembered.

That's all.

A GIRL

A girl,
younger than me.

About 8 years less
than that

of what I am.

She's attracted to me.

To my soul.
To my style.

The way I speak
and think.

The way I move
and walk.

She has feelings
for me.

I have feelings
for her.

She moves me.

She's got me

where she wants me.

The other night,
together in the room.

Laying on the bed.

Sober
but drunk off infatuation.

She ask,
out of the blue.

"How many women
have you dated?

How many women
have you made feel special—alive?"

I paused for a second
(to think about it)

but did not
hesitate to answer.

"About thirty, you?"

She frowns in shock
but also

she was not

too surprised.
She clears her throat.

"Me, about four or five?"

"Well, I'd like to be six,"

I say
as my fingers

run through her hair.

"I'd like that, too
but I don't want to be

your thirty-first."

"Don't see it like that,
my love.

That only means
I've had thirty lessons.

More experience
with relationships.

More experience
with people

and loss.

More life.
More breath.

More feelings exchanged.

A better human.
A better lover…

for you."

WHAT COUNTS

I'm sorry,
but I don't have

the time
to save you

or the world.

I'm too busy
making sense

of the stars
in my head.

Too busy
writing my own story.

And too busy
making sure

I don't forget
what counts.

FOREVER

Sometimes
what hurts

never quite
fully heals.

Sometimes
what hurts

stays deep
within the back

of our hearts
forever.

THINGS FOR YOU

We all need
some kind

of closure sometimes.

Something,
anything.

A sign.
A person.
A place.
A memory.

Something
to remind us

that it's okay
to let go.

That it's okay
to move on.

We all need this
revelation sometimes.

We deserve peace
from the past
and hope in the future.

We deserve
so much more

than we think
we do.

Life is love
and love is life

and sometimes
we must learn

to leave
certain things

behind…
in order

to progress
and grow.

The meaning of it all
is simple.

We must always
welcome the end

of things
in order

to welcome

the beginning.

From people
to jobs

to friends,
family

and places.

Nothing lasts forever
but it is up to us

to take
the concept of forever

and make it
last long enough

while we're
still here.

That is what
makes us beautiful.

The fact
that we all

have the ability

to close a door

while opening
a new one.

Even when
we don't know

what is really
going on.

So this is me
telling you,

it's okay.

Wherever this life
takes you—takes us.

Together or not.
It's okay.

It's okay
to loosen your grip

from my hand.

It's okay
to take a few more
steps than me.

It's okay
to not look back

and say good-bye.

To not remember.

To not want
to come back

to where you belong.

It's okay…
and I understand

how it works.

So let this be
what you've been

looking for.

Let this be
the answer

to all those questions
that have been

keeping you up
at night.

It's okay
and I hope

whatever you decide
to do

is

*the right thing
for you.*

GOOD THINGS

Good things come
when you unlock

your heart.

Even on the worst
of days,

good things
happen

when you start
your day

with coffee.

ALL ALONG

What's yours
will find you.

So I wouldn't worry
about anything else.

I wouldn't worry
about being alone

for now.

Your love
is your love

and if they're
meant for you,

then one day
you'll be reunited

again.

One day
they'll find you

and tell you
how much

they've missed you
all along.

It always happens
like this.

It never fails.

FOLLOW IT

Some people live
these terribly confused lives.

Spread positivity
online

but in real life
they hate.

They destroy.

They complain
and are never happy

with themselves.

Some people
live these sad lives,

therefore,

you should never
believe everything

you see.

Follow your heart
at all cost.

It sense things
you can't see.

It knows better
than you think.

HEAL HERE

Be protective
of you

and your feelings.

You don't have to
cut yourself

short

because you care
about them.

You don't have to
give in

or change

because you love them
either.

Do you.
Be you.

Find
what makes you

happy.

Grow there.
Love there.

Heal there.

BETTER ALONE

If you see
the person

you hurt
happy,

then by all means
leave them alone.

They obviously
moved on

and don't need you.

It's harsh
but true.

Leave them alone.

They're better off
without you.

Better off
being alone.

Sometimes
things just don't
work out.

REMEMBER THAT

You have to save
a little inspiration.

A little light
inside.

You have to
save it

but not for anyone
you love

or anyone
you want to save

but for
yourself.

You have to
keep it safe.

That little spark.

That little sense
of change,

of self.

You have to
protect it

at all cost
and use it

when all else
fails.

Use it
when you're pinned

against the ropes.

Believe me,
that little bit

of inspiration
is priceless.

It can really
pull you out

of the gutter
when nothing else can.

It can really
turn things around.

It can really
give you

what you need
when you feel

most alone,
you know?

Keep you company,
you know?

Sometimes
a little bit

of inspiration
is all you need.

The darkness
is still

the darkness
but it is not

all dark
with just a little

glimmer
of hope—of
light.

Always
remember that.

MOVE ON

Don't hate them.

Pray for the people
who've hurt you.

Learn
from what they've

caused you
and move on.

IF IT KILLS US

You say
you have had

enough

but even when
you have been pushed

to your limits
you find the strength

within you
to carry on.

To push forward.

To laugh
even if the odds

are against you.

To love
when you feel

alone.

The light
goes through you.

*It is born
of you*

and from you.

And the fire
continues to flame

within you.

I can see it.

I can relate to it.
It makes me

feel better
about myself.

About how I feel.

I am not alone
and neither are you.

We have been broken
and say

we will never
love again

and still,

we meet
new people.

And still,
we admire them.

And still,
we fall in love

with them
and lose ourselves

in-between.

Over and over again.

There is no end.

We say
we have had

enough
but we search

and search
and search.

And we will continue
to search

no matter how bad

it gets.

No matter how much
it hurts.

People like us
want to save others.

Want to love.

And we will never
stop doing so,

even if it kills us.

We arrive
for them

because we do not know
what to do

other than that.

It's in our blood.

There's no other way
to say it.

It is
what it is.

LIVES CHANGE

That's how
it is sometimes.

You do wrong
to the wrong people.

You unintentionally
hurt them.

You do things
you never thought

you would
and in an instant

lives change.

Lovers
become strangers.

Friends
become memories

flowing
through the wind.

LET IT BE

Pay attention
to the way

you feel
when they

walk away.

By then,
you will know

if your heart
gets filled with

relief or sorrow.

If you feel
relief,

then for Christ's sake
never call that person

again.

If you feel
great sorrow

then it only means

you have someone
worth missing.

Hold on to them...

a feeling like that
is only

as kind
and beautiful

as you let it

be.

WHAT COUNTS

We have all
lost something

dear to us.

A relationship.
A job.

An opportunity.
An idea...

but it is
the way

we overcome it
that counts.

What we learn
and what we

decide to do
from there

on out.

IGNORE THEMSELVES

Everyone
is too busy

trying to be
someone else.

Trying to impress
someone else.

Working
for someone else

and perhaps
even

living
for someone else,

too.

So do not worry
about losing

your sense
of self for now.

Everyone has got
some kind

of burden
they're living through.

Some kind
of war.

Some kind
of trouble.

Some kind
of life

they'd love
to change.

Love to have.

Everyone wants
to be someone

but everyone
is too busy

ignoring
themselves.

WHAT I THOUGHT

I want you
but I'm not ready.

The same way

I want to move on
and let go

but the past
is a lot heavier

than
I thought.

DO NOT BE

Do not be
ashamed

of who you are.

Of what interests you.

Of what
brings you peace.

Your skin
is your skin

and your heart
is your heart.

And what you feel
is real.

Don't question it.

Don't be afraid
of what your soul

is telling you.

Of what your heart
really wants.

If you
don't want something

anymore
then it is okay

to leave it
behind.

It is okay
to let it go.

No matter who
you hurt.

You have to do
what is meant

for you.

Follow
your own path.

Be
your own guide

and hold
your own hand

sometimes.

Your life
is your life.

Your mind
is your mind.

Find your purpose.

Find it.

And never stop
chasing it.

Never stop
believing in yourself.

And never stop
collecting

what you've lost.

Everyone needs
to be

reminded of this.

Because sometimes
life gets

so hard... that
it makes us all

forget

what we deserve.

Makes us all
forget

who we really are.

Feel it
then hold on to it.

Know it.
Know it.
Know it.

MY SOUL

Sometimes
that's all

I want.

A little time.
A little company.

You give me
your heart,

and baby,
I swear

to give you
my soul.

THE ONLY ONE

I know
commitment

is a difficult thing
to do.

And I don't mean
committing

to someone
or a relationship.

No
it's deeper than that.

I mean
pledging

to your own
happiness.

Sticking
to what brings you

peace.

To what brings you
laughter.

To the things
that make you

a better person.

Commitment
is such

a hard thing
to do...

but I will
tell you this

with the stars
in my soul

and the holiness
in my heart,

and I will not
sugarcoat it

because

it is not
in my nature

to do so.

Commit

to yourself.

Devote
to yourself.

Dedicate your time
to yourself

and *fuck*
anything else.

It is
a bittersweet thing

to do
but in the end,

when all has passed
and the bullshit

has cleared
the sky.

The only person
you have

to prove yourself to...
is you.

The only person
you have

to make proud...
is you.

Day by day.
Night by night.

And pushing through
the grain

in-between.

Your life
is your life

and the best kind
of love

you can ever
receive

is the one
only you

can give
to yourself.

PEOPLE YOU LOVE

*What good
is anything*

*and everything
if it is*

*not spent
with the people*

you love.

FROM THE START

Why is it
so hard

to make it
work with you.

So hard
to talk to you,

to open up
with you.

I don't know why
but it feels

so goddamn heavy
inside.

I don't know why
but I miss you

even when
you're with me.

I miss
who we were,

what we had,

before
we let

what we felt
get in the way.

I wish
I could go back.

I wish
I could take it

from the start.

*Enjoy the people
you love*

while you have them.

The past is haunting.

And the future
is hard to swallow.

Make it all count.

Make it all
worth remembering.

ENERGY IS EVERYTHING

Understand
that energy

is everything
and everything

is energy.

And what you
put out

and let in
affects your world.

Our world.

Protect your energy
at all cost.

Protect your heart
and soul,

for none of them
can be destroyed

and none of them
should be tamed down.

There is power
in what you feel.

Power
in what you love

and how you
share love.

Power
in your words

and actions.

In your thoughts
and being.

You are
what you feel.

What you say.
What you

present
to yourself

when you're alone.

You are
you

and what you feel
can sometimes be

the most powerful
thing

in the world.

Stay positive,
my sweet people.

Your energy
is everything.

THE OLD YOU

I miss
the old you

and you miss
the old me.

Maybe
we're still living

in the past.

Maybe
we're still looking

for what we lost
when we let go…

instead
of looking

for what's missing
within

ourselves.

JUST HOLD ON

Sometimes
you can't find

what you lost
in the same place

you lost it.

The same way
you can't find

love
in those

who left you
to die—alone

and cold.

That's not
how it works.

You're never
going to heal

if you keep
running back.

You're never
going to let go,

if all you do
is hold on.

Hands get tired.
Hearts get exhausted.

Minds get overworked.
And energy gets depleted.

Let go.
Let live.
Let heal.

I promise you
things will get better.

Just keep moving forward.

There is no need
to go back

to the start.

ANY OTHER WAY

I drown
the people

I care about.

I over
nurture them.

I over
love them.

Overthink them.

I push away

or

bring them closer.

I'm sorry.

I love
until it hurts.

I don't know
any other

way.

"THE SCIENCE OF…" SERIES
IS COMING SOON - SPRING OF 2020